COOL
Cutting Edge
CAREERS

MARINE BIOLOGIST

By William David Thomas

Content Adviser: Amanda L. Southwood, Ph.D.,
Department of Biology & Marine Biology, University of North Carolina Wilmington

Gareth Stevens
Publishing

Please visit our web site at **www.garethstevens.com.**
For a free catalog describing Gareth Stevens Publishing's list of high-quality books,
call 1-800-542-2595 (USA) or 1-800-387-3178 (Canada).
Gareth Stevens Publishing's fax: 1-877-542-2596

Library of Congress Cataloging-in-Publication Data
Thomas, William David.
    Marine biologist / by William David Thomas.
        p. cm. — (Cool careers: cutting edge)
    Includes bibliographical references and index.
        ISBN-10: 1-4339-1957-5   ISBN-13: 978-1-4339-1957-2 (lib. bdg.)
        ISBN-10: 1-4339-2156-1   ISBN-13: 978-1-4339-2156-8 (soft cover)
        1. Marine biologists—Vocational guidance—Juvenile literature. 2. Marine biology—
Juvenile literature. I. Title. .
    QH91.45.T457   2010
    578.77023—dc22   2009000239

This edition first published in 2010 by
Gareth Stevens Publishing
A Weekly Reader® Company
1 Reader's Digest Rd.
Pleasantville, NY 10570-7000 USA

Copyright © 2010 by Gareth Stevens, Inc.

Executive Managing Editor: Lisa M. Herrington
Senior Editor: Brian Fitzgerald
Senior Designer: Keith Plechaty
Produced by Editorial Directions, Inc.
Art Direction and Page Production: Paula Jo Smith Design

Picture credits: Cover, title page, © Mark A. Johnson/Alamy; p. 5 © David Fleetham/Alamy;
p. 7 © Images&Stories/Alamy; p. 8 © Image Source Pink/Alamy; p. 10 © Nature Picture
Library/Alamy; p. 11 Brownie Harris/Corbis; p. 12 Bettman/Corbis; p. 14 Kevin Palmer/
Seapics.com; p. 15 Steve Adams, Marine Careers Project, University of New Hampshire;
p. 16 © David Shale/naturepl.com; p. 17 © David Shale/naturepl.com; p. 18 Mark Conlin/
Alamy; p. 19 © Woods Hole Oceanographic Institution; p. 21 © Liz Brooks, Woods Hole
Oceanographic Institution; p. 22 © Jim West/Alamy; p. 25 © Ted Spiegel/Corbis; p. 27
(top) Steve Adams, Marine Careers Project, University of New Hampshire; p. 27 (bottom)
Stephen Frink Collection/Alamy

Printed in the United States of America

1 2 3 4 5 6 7 8 9 14 13 12 11 10 09

CONTENTS

Words in the glossary appear in **bold** type the first time they are used in the text.

CHAPTER 1

SHARKS AND SATELLITES

A newspaper reporter leans over the edge of the boat. He is holding onto the fins of a shark that is about 6 feet (1.8 meters) long. Suddenly, the shark twists and snaps its jaws. "Keep your arm in tight," Carl Meyer tells the reporter. "They can come right around and reach [you]."

Playing Tag With Sharks

The reporter is learning about Meyer's work. Meyer is a **marine biologist** in Hawaii. He studies plants and animals that live in the ocean. His special area of study is sharks.

In his work, Meyer catches sharks and puts electronic tags on them. The tags record the sharks' movements and swimming patterns. After a set time, the tags come off and float to the ocean's surface. The tags send the information to a satellite. Meyer then downloads that information to his computer.

Marine biologists sometimes have to do dangerous work. They tag sharks like these in Hawaii.

Scientists once thought that sharks stayed in a small area. Meyer has found that sharks travel up to 700 miles (1,127 kilometers) across oceans. He also learned that some sharks gather in groups during certain times of the month. He doesn't know why that happens. To find out, he will keep tagging sharks.

What Do Marine Biologists Do?

Marine biologists study all living things in the ocean, from huge whales to tiny **bacteria**. They often work from ships and small boats. Marine biologists may swim or dive to collect plants and animals to study. They often take photographs underwater.

On land, marine biologists use computers, microscopes, and testing equipment. These tools help them study the plants and animals they collect. They must write reports and keep detailed records of their work.

NOAA

Many marine biologists work for the National Oceanic and Atmospheric Administration (NOAA). NOAA scientists study oceans, coasts, and the air around Earth. Their work includes weather forecasts, storm warnings, and weather study. The agency works to protect areas along coasts from pollution and damage. NOAA also studies and regulates **fisheries**.

Do you like being in the water? Some marine biologists go beneath the surface to collect information.

Some marine biologists teach at colleges or universities. Others work for businesses or government agencies. A few work at aquariums or marine animal parks.

Scuba

Scuba stands for "self-contained underwater breathing apparatus." Scuba divers wear a mask, swim flippers, and a tank of compressed gas. The gas is a mixture of oxygen and nitrogen. Two **regulators** control the gas.

In modern scuba gear, the first regulator is on the air tank. It lowers the gas pressure to a safe level. The gas goes through a thin hose to a mouthpiece. The second regulator is on the mouthpiece. It lowers the pressure even more and lets the diver breathe in. A special rubber flap in the mouthpiece lets the diver breathe out without letting water in.

What You'll Need

To work in marine biology, you'll need to know a lot about underwater life. You must be skilled with math and computers. You should be a good swimmer and a trained scuba diver. Experience with large and small boats is helpful, too.

How to Become a Marine Biologist

All marine biologists need a four-year college degree. They study marine life, chemistry, math, and computers. Most marine biologists specialize in one area, such as sea mammals. That requires a master's degree and another two years of study. Many research and teaching positions require a doctoral degree, or Ph.D. That can take up to five more years of study.

Could You Be a Marine Biologist?

If you think you'd like to be a marine biologist, ask yourself these questions:

- Do you like science, math, and computers?
- Are you interested in plants and animals that live in water?
- Are you a good swimmer?
- Do you like being in boats?

If so, being a marine biologist may be the right career for you!

CHAPTER 2

IN THE LAB

The sea squirt is not an exciting animal. It doesn't swim or jump. It isn't beautiful. James McClintock says it is "a spongelike, bloblike **organism** that sits on the ocean bottom and doesn't move." Someday, however, the sea squirt may save people's lives.

Studying Invertebrates

McClintock specializes in **invertebrates**, animals with no backbone. He studies living things "that cannot get up and run away when something is trying to eat them." Sea squirts can't move, but somehow they protect themselves from other creatures. McClintock wondered how they do it. To find out, he spent hundreds of hours working in labs.

Sea squirts live on the bottom of the ocean.

A marine biologist in the lab examines an invertebrate called a sea star.

Useful Chemicals

In his lab work, McClintock learned that the sea squirt makes chemicals inside its body. The chemicals protect it from animals wanting to eat it. After a lot of work, McClintock identified a chemical compound in sea

Underwater Explorer

Jacques Cousteau (1910–1997) inspired many young people to become marine biologists. He was a French naval officer and an inventor. He loved the sea and its creatures. He helped invent the Aqua-Lung. This was the first modern equipment to let divers breathe underwater. Cousteau explored the sea and wrote about sea animals. He made TV shows and films as well. He built a ship called *Calypso* and sailed it around the world. Everywhere he stopped, Cousteau talked about the ocean. He worked to protect sea animals and to stop pollution.

Cousteau (center) wearing scuba gear

squirts. This special compound may help fight a type of skin cancer. These little bloblike animals may actually help cancer patients beat this disease.

Collecting sea squirts is hard, however. This type of sea squirt lives only in Antarctica, the coldest place on Earth. McClintock dives under the icy waters to collect them. Other Antarctic animals sometimes dive with him. "Swimming with penguins," he says, "is one of the most spectacular things you could ever imagine."

Answering Questions

Like other scientists, marine biologists do a lot of research. They examine sea plants and animals to answer questions. Why are the shells of these turtle eggs so thin? Why are these fish dying? Why is that seaweed growing so fast? How does the sea squirt protect itself?

Marine biologists examine **specimens** to find answers. These may be tiny bacteria or large fish. They **dissect** the specimens. Marine biologists take blood to test. They use microscopes to examine scales, skin, and plant cells.

A marine biologist may put colored dyes in the specimens. This makes tiny body parts easier to see. Biologists use chemical tests and X-rays, too. They use computers to collect and store information.

Paperwork

Marine biologists do a lot of writing. They must carefully record their lab work. They may publish their research reports in science journals. Everyone in the field reads these journals to learn about new research.

Marine biologists also write requests for money to pay for their projects. These payments are called

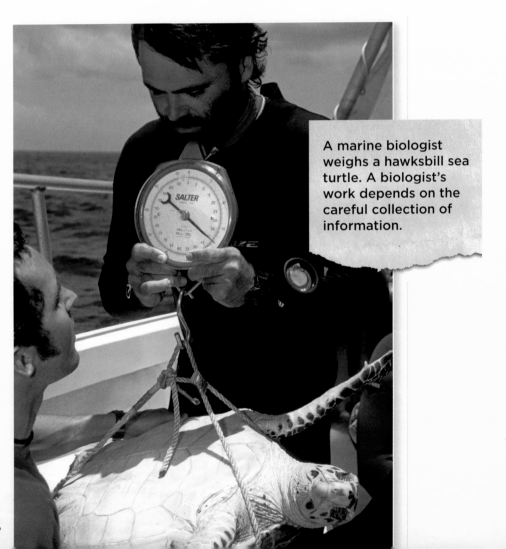

A marine biologist weighs a hawksbill sea turtle. A biologist's work depends on the careful collection of information.

grants. The government or a business will often pay for research. The marine biologists carry out the research project. Then, they must write reports on the results and on how the money was spent.

On the Job: Marine Microbiologist

Micro means "small." Marine microbiology is the study of the tiniest ocean creatures. These ocean creatures might be small, but they're also important. Scientists have learned that some **algae** make a kind of oil that could be a source of energy in the future.

Russell Hill teaches at the University of Maryland. He collects and tests ocean bacteria. Hill hopes that his work will lead to new drugs to treat diseases such as malaria. He spends most of his time in classrooms and labs. However, he says, "I spend a few weeks each year doing research cruises to collect [specimens]."

CHAPTER 3

IN THE OCEANS

More than two-thirds of Earth's surface is covered by oceans. Many parts of oceans are still unexplored. New creatures are still being discovered. The oceans may be huge, but they are easily damaged. Marine biologists work to protect the seas and sea life.

Deep-Sea Discoveries

The Mid-Atlantic Ridge is an underwater mountain range. It rises from the ocean bottom where the water is 2 miles (3.2 km) deep. In 2007, a team of scientists went to look at the ridge. They used remotely operated vehicles (ROVs) to explore.

Cameras on the ROVs got pictures of a see-through ball covered with polka dots. It was a glass squid! They photographed a viperfish with needle-sharp

Scientists found glass squids (above) and viperfish (left) in the deep sea.

teeth. Scientists found hundreds of other interesting specimens.

Marine biologists are studying these strange deep-sea creatures. They want to learn as much as they can about the ocean and what lives in it.

A Thorny Problem

Coral reefs are found near the surface of warm, tropical oceans. They are home to millions of different kinds of fish and other creatures. Corals are tiny living animals. Their skeletons form the hard, stony reefs. Coral reefs can be huge. They supply food and shelter to the creatures in and around the coral.

A crown of thorns feeds on a coral reef. Marine biologists work to protect this important part of the ocean.

Today, coral reefs are being destroyed. In many places, a spiny sea star called the crown of thorns is eating them. Marine biologists in Australia discovered a poison. It kills the sea star but does not harm other sea life.

Global Warming

Another danger to coral reefs is **global warming**. Warmer sea temperatures can cause **coral bleaching**. The warmer water causes the coral to turn white, often killing it. Some reefs near Florida are turning white. So are large parts of the Great Barrier Reef, a 1,250-mile-long (2,012 km) reef near Australia. If the coral reefs die, so will the creatures that live there.

Marine biologists around the world are measuring ocean temperatures. They work from ships and small boats. They also use **thermal** images taken by satellites in space. These images show warm and cold areas. The pictures are used to find areas where the ocean is getting warmer.

Alvin

Alvin is a deep-sea **submersible**. It was developed by the U.S. Navy and scientists at the Woods Hole Oceanographic Institution (WHOI) in Massachusetts.

Alvin lets marine biologists and other scientists go places where they could never go before. It can dive up to 2.8 miles (4.5 km) beneath the surface of the sea. It can carry three people. The vessel has bright lights, cameras, and arms for collecting specimens. Scientists have used *Alvin* to discover hundreds of new kinds of sea creatures.

On the Job: Marine Biologist Liz Brooks

Liz Brooks works for the fisheries section of the National Oceanic and Atmospheric Administration (NOAA). Her research helps set rules for the fishing trade.

Q: How do you collect information?
Brooks: I participate in research cruises at sea. The scientists help sort the fish that come up in the **trawl net**. We weigh and measure the fish, examine stomach contents, [and] determine sex. [We use computer programs.] Then we make an estimate of the future population of each fish **species**.

Q: What's the best thing about your job?
Brooks: Knowing that the work I do has a direct benefit to society.

Q: What's the worst thing?
Brooks: The work I do is used to determine how many fish can be caught in the coming years. This directly affects the income of people who catch the fish.

Q: Why did you want to become a marine biologist?
Brooks: I always enjoyed the outdoors. I wanted to understand how things worked, why things changed.

Liz Brooks holds a huge monkfish on the deck of a boat.

Q: What is the most exciting assignment you've ever had?

Brooks: Traveling to Japan to work with scientists from all over the world. We were trying to determine the [condition] of several large sharks.

Q: What would you tell a young person thinking about a career in marine biology?

Brooks: Study math! It will be valuable to anyone who wants to be a scientist.

CHAPTER 4

IN LAKES AND RIVERS

Freshwater is a very valuable resource. Many places in the world, including parts of the United States, don't have enough of it. **Limnologists** are scientists who study plants and animals that live in freshwater. Like marine biologists, they study water life, among other things.

Invasion!

The Great Lakes hold more than 20 percent of the world's freshwater. **Invasive species** are a big problem. These plants or animals are brought from other places. They spread quickly and drive out native species.

Zebra mussels are one of these invaders. They look like small clams with stripes on their shells. They were first found in the Great Lakes in 1988. Zebra mussels are native to Russia.

Zebra mussels multiply quickly. They also live very close together. Zebra mussels attach themselves to hard surfaces, such as rocks or metal pipes. Some of these pipes supply drinking water to cities. The mussels clog the pipes and slow the flow of water.

Zebra mussel shells cover a piece of a wooden dock from Lake Erie in Michigan.

Biologists have learned that special paint can help. Paint containing copper or tin stops the mussel buildup. People must now clean the bottoms of their boats to help stop the spread of zebra mussels.

Deadly Skies

Acid rain is a growing problem around the world. It is caused by gases that come from car engines and coal-burning power plants. These gases mix with water in the air. The result is acid rain.

Acid rain damages small lakes most easily. There are many of these in the Adirondack Mountains of New York. One state worker there said, "Some of these lakes are crystal clear. They're beautiful, but they are absolutely dead. No fish. No plants. No insects. Acid rain killed them."

The way to stop acid rain is to stop burning coal and gasoline. Biologists are looking for other ways to help. Scientists in New York learned that brook trout stay healthier than other trout in water with high acid levels. Now they are trying to find out why. It may be possible to breed trout that can live with acid rain.

Biologists are also trying to lower the acid level in streams and lakes damaged by acid rain. One way is to

On the Job: Marine Mammal Response Manager

You may have seen bumper stickers that read "Save the Whales." That's what Edward Lyman does. Whales often get tangled in fishing lines, nets, and ropes. Lyman helps rescue these whales. He also studies whale behavior to learn why they get tangled in nets. He follows **pods** of whales as they swim from Hawaii to Alaska in the summer. Lyman says, "It is extremely rewarding to save an animal or learn something that might save other animals in the future."

How much has acid rain damaged this lake's plants and animals? A limnologist checks the water in New York's Woods Lake.

put lime in them. Lime is a powder made by crushing and burning a rock called limestone.

Dawn Kirk is a fisheries biologist in Virginia. She found one stream where there were no fish. She and her team tested the water. Its acid level was high. So the scientists added lime. "We carried [trout] up and restocked that section with native fish," she said. "And they did great."

It takes a lot of lime to correct acid in water. It can only be done in streams and small lakes. Limnologists are still searching for other ways to fight acid rain.

CHAPTER 5

FROM AQUARIUMS TO CLASSROOMS

There are lots of different kinds of jobs for marine biologists. Some are at sea. Some are on land. Many jobs combine the two.

Aquarium Keepers

Many large cities have aquariums. These are like zoos for sea animals. Most aquarium keepers are trained marine biologists. They are responsible for the health and safety of all the animals. They try to keep the aquariums as much like the sea as possible. Being an aquarium keeper is like managing your own private ocean.

Marine Biology Technicians

Marine biology technicians keep equipment clean, tested, and working properly. They may take care of live specimens in special tanks. The tank water must be checked for temperature and cleanliness. Technicians also must know what each animal eats.

These marine biologists work for an aquarium. They are collecting sea stars and other creatures for the tanks.

Alex Almario is an operations technician. He works for the Environmental Protection Agency in Florida. Almario collects water, plant, and animal specimens. He takes care of boats, scuba gear, and lab equipment.

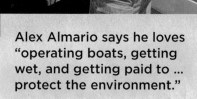

Alex Almario says he loves "operating boats, getting wet, and getting paid to ... protect the environment."

Teachers

Some marine biologists teach others. Maryellen Timmons works at the Marine Education Center and Aquarium in Savannah, Georgia. Her students range in age from kindergarten to college. She teaches in classrooms and on ships. "I love to see ... the excitement in students," Timmons says, "when they learn about marine science and how it affects their lives."

Songs of the Sea

Many marine biologists find a special area of interest. Some study the songs of whales. They use underwater recorders to capture the music. Computers help the biologists find patterns in the sounds. They have found that humpback whale songs can last for 30 minutes. The whales sing them exactly the same way, over and over again.

Some marine biologists think whales use songs to communicate with one another. Others believe males sing to attract females. Whale songs are still a mystery of the sea.

MARINE BIOLOGIST

OUTLOOK

- In 2006, about 87,000 biological scientists, including marine biologists, were working in the United States. By 2016, there will be about 95,000.

- Some marine biologists teach at colleges or universities. Others work for businesses or government agencies. A smaller number of them work at aquariums or marine animal parks.

WHAT YOU'LL DO

- Marine biologists collect and study plants and animals that live in water. They use lab equipment to examine and test these specimens.

- Marine biologists write reports and keep detailed records of their work.

- Marine biologists sometimes work from ships and small boats. They swim or dive to study or collect marine life.

WHAT YOU'LL NEED

- All marine biologists need a bachelor's degree. Most marine biologists also have a master's degree or a doctoral degree.

- You should be a strong swimmer and a trained scuba diver.

WHAT YOU'LL EARN

- In 2006, beginning marine biologists earned about $52,000. Those with experience and doctoral degrees earned as much as $94,000.

Source: U.S. Department of Labor, Bureau of Labor Statistics, and the Commission on Professionals in Science and Technology

GLOSSARY

acid rain — rain containing gases from car engines and coal-burning plants that damages the environment

algae — plants made of one or more cells; seaweed is one kind of algae

bacteria — microscopic living things

coral bleaching — the loss of a coral's color, often caused by warm seawater

dissect — to cut up a dead animal in order to study it

fisheries — places where fish are caught or raised for sale

global warming — the slow rise in worldwide temperatures

invasive species — plants or animals from other places that spread quickly and drive out native species

invertebrates — animals with no backbone

limnologists — scientists who study plants and animals that live in freshwater

marine biologist — a scientist who studies plants and animals that live in the ocean

organism — any living thing

pods — groups of whales

regulators — devices on scuba tanks that control the flow of air to the diver

species — a group of similar animals or plants

specimens — samples taken for scientific study

submersible — a small underwater craft

thermal — having to do with heat

trawl net — a large net that a boat drags along the sea bottom

TO FIND OUT MORE

Books

Conlan, Kathy. *Under the Ice: A Marine Biologist at Work*. Toronto: Kids Can Press, 2008.

Thompson, Lisa. *Sea Life Scientist: Have You Got What It Takes to Be a Marine Biologist?* Minneapolis: Compass Point Books, 2008.

Unwin, Mike. *Secrets of the Deep: Marine Biologists*. Chicago: Heinemann Library, 2008.

Zronik, John. *Jacques Cousteau: Conserving Underwater Worlds*. New York: Crabtree Publishing, 2007.

Web Sites

British Broadcasting Corporation: The Blue Planet
www.bbc.co.uk/nature/blueplanet/blue/master.shtml
Try answering these questions about the oceans.

Lawrence Hall of Science: Whale Sounds
www.lawrencehallofscience.org/whale
Listen to the songs and see the sound patterns of different whales.

Sea Grant: Marine Careers
www.marinecareers.net
Find out about marine biology and other ocean careers.

Weird Fins
www.nmfs.noaa.gov/rss/podcasts/weirdfins
Learn some strange fish facts from the National Marine Fisheries Service at NOAA.

INDEX

About the Author

William David Thomas lives in Rochester, New York. He works in public education. Bill has written software manuals, books for children and young adults, and a few poems. Bill sends his sincere thanks to Steve Adams, webmaster for the Marine Careers project at the University of New Hampshire, for his kind assistance with this book.